Explore the
coral Reef

FIRST EDITION
Series Editor Deborah Lock; **US Senior Editor** Shannon Beatty; **Editor** Arpita Nath;
Design Assistant Sadie Thomas; **Art Editor** Dheeraj Arora; **Senior Art Editor** Tory Gordon-Harris;
Producer Sara Hu; **Pre-Production Producer** Nadine King; **Jacket Designer** Natalie Godwin;
Managing Editor Soma Chowdhury; **Managing Art Editor** Ahlawat Gunjan;
Art Directors Rachel Foster and Martin Wilson; **Reading Consultant** Linda Gambrell, PhD

THIS EDITION
Editorial Management by Oriel Square
Produced for DK by WonderLab Group LLC
Jennifer Emmett, Erica Green, Kate Hale, *Founders*

Editors Grace Hill Smith, Libby Romero, Michaela Weglinski;
Photography Editors Kelley Miller, Annette Kiesow, Nicole DiMella;
Managing Editor Rachel Houghton; **Designers** Project Design Company; **Researcher** Michelle Harris;
Copy Editor Lori Merritt; **Indexer** Connie Binder; **Proofreader** Larry Shea;
Reading Specialist Dr. Jennifer Albro; **Curriculum Specialist** Elaine Larson

Published in the United States by DK Publishing
1745 Broadway, 20th Floor, New York, NY 10019

Copyright © 2023 Dorling Kindersley Limited
DK, a Division of Penguin Random House LLC
23 24 25 26 27 10 9 8 7 6 5 4 3 2 1
001–333457–Apr/2023

A catalog record for this book
is available from the Library of Congress.
HC ISBN: 978-0-7440-6799-6
PB ISBN: 978-0-7440-6800-9

DK books are available at special discounts when purchased
in bulk for sales promotions, premiums, fundraising, or
educational use. For details, contact: DK Publishing Special Markets,
1745 Broadway, 20th Floor, New York, NY 10019
SpecialSales@dk.com

Printed and bound in China

The publisher would like to thank the following for their kind permission to reproduce their images:
a=above; c=center; b=below; l=left; r=right; t=top; b/g=background

Dorling Kindersley: Tina Gong 10c; **Dreamstime.com:** Luca Gialdini 20, Ingrid Prats / Titania1980 3;
Getty Images / iStock: strmko 4-5; **Shutterstock.com:** Sergius Bleicher 24-25, Rich Carey 10-11, Diman_Diver 21,
Rostislav Stefanek 26-27, Stock for you 19cra
Cover images: *Front:* **Dreamstime.com:** John Anderson b, Artisticco Llc; *Back:* **Dreamstime.com:** Andrii Symonenko bl
All other images © Dorling Kindersley

For the curious
www.dk.com

Explore the
coral Reef

Deborah Lock

Contents

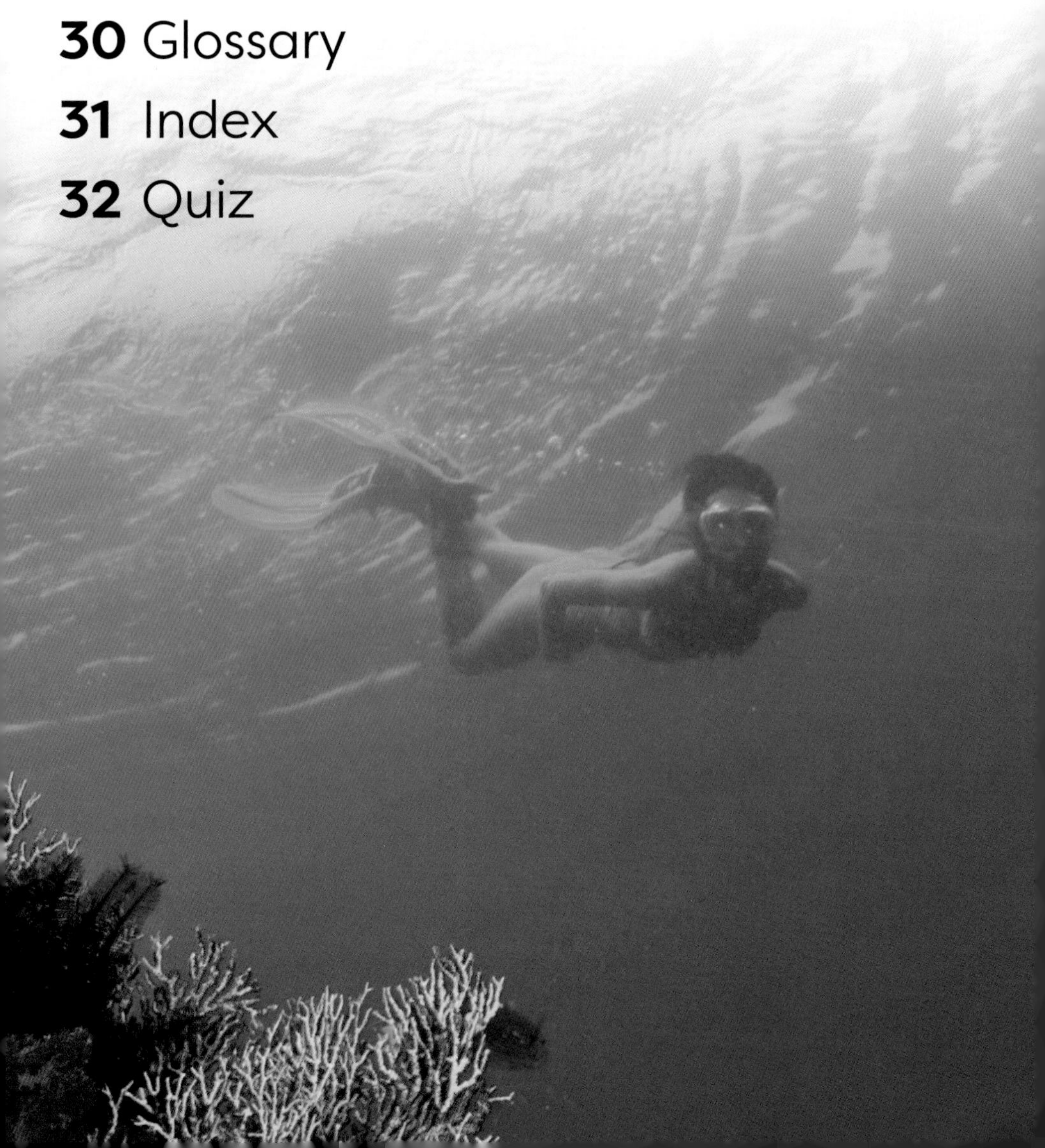

Coral

Here is a coral reef.

What animals do you see?

coral

fish

Sea Turtles

The sea turtles play in the ocean.

shell

flipper

Seahorses

The seahorses sway to and fro.

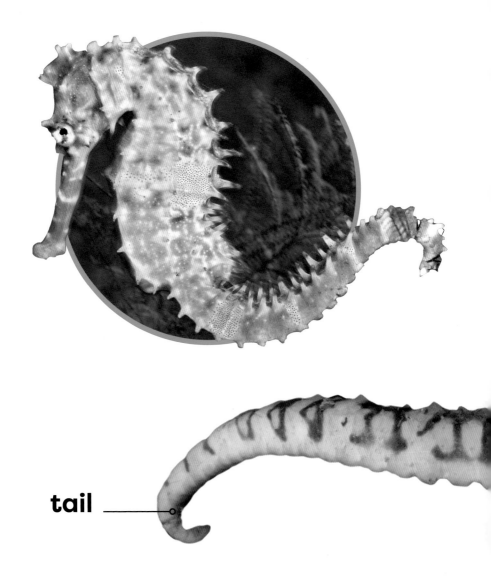

tail

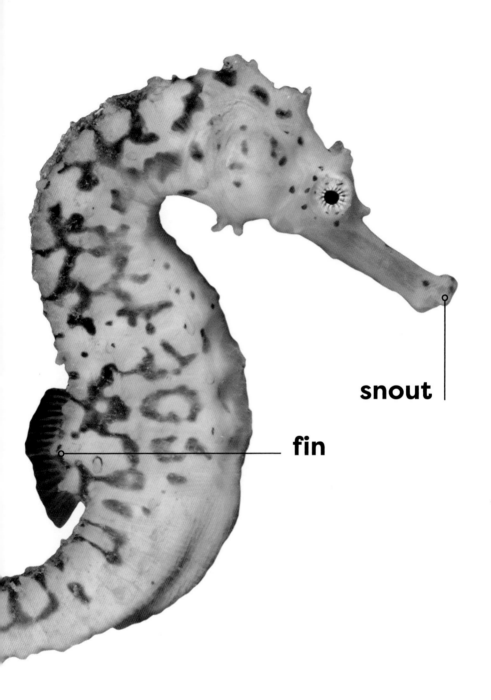

snout

fin

arm

Sea Stars

Sea stars crawl
on the ocean floor.

Jellyfish

Jellyfish float
up and down
in the ocean.

tentacles

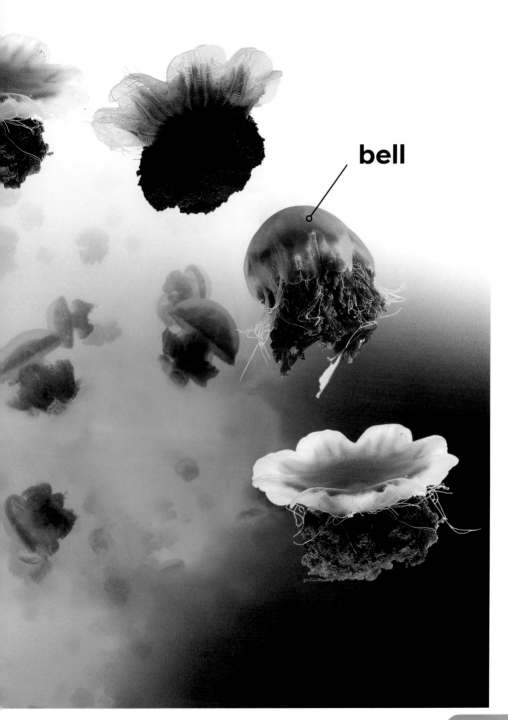

bell

tail

Sharks

Here comes a shark.
It looks for food.

fin

mouth

Octopuses

An octopus shoots off
to hide.

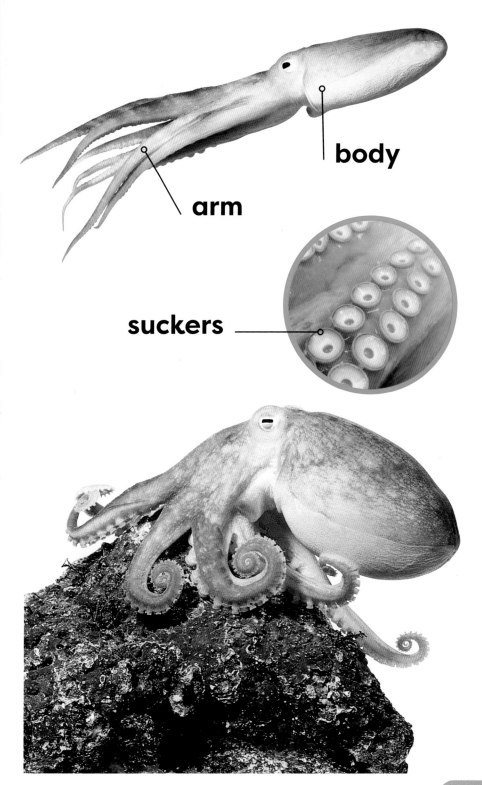

body

arm

suckers

Crabs

Crabs hide in
the coral and
inside big shells.

shell

leg

claw

Rays

A ray hides on
the ocean floor.

tail

hiding

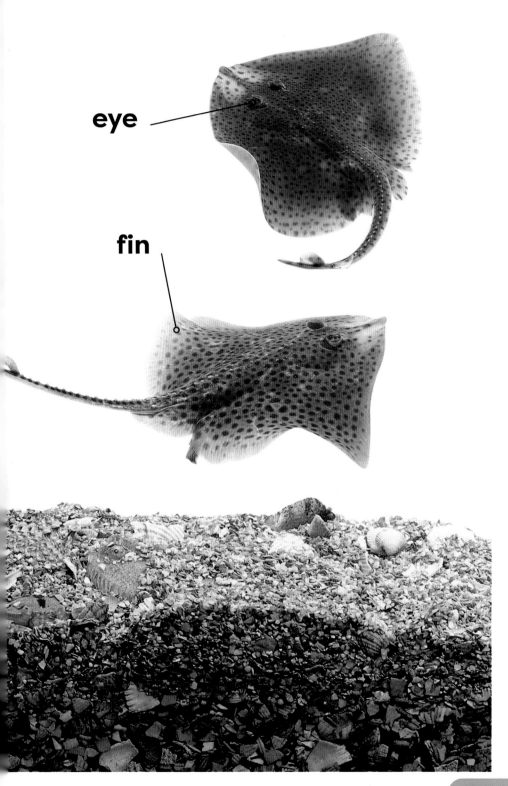

eye

fin

Dolphins

A dolphin swims away.
It moves its tail
up and down.

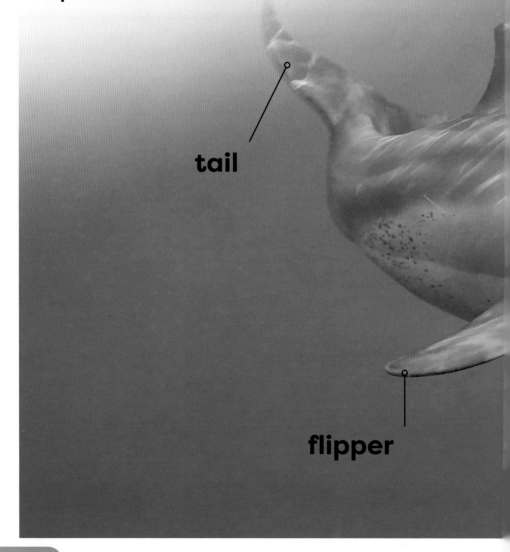

tail

flipper

mouth

Eels

An eel looks out for the shark.

eye

fin

tail

The shark swims away.

gills

nose

Glossary

eel
a snake-like fish

octopus
a sea animal with eight long arms

ray
a flat fish with large wing-like fins

sea star
a sea animal with five arms shaped like a star

sea turtle
a marine reptile with a domed shell

Index

Quiz

Answer the questions to see what you have learned. Check your answers with an adult.

Which sea animal am I?

1. I have flippers and a hard shell.

2. I have a bell and tentacles.

3. I have long arms covered in suckers.

4. I hide in coral and inside big shells.

5. I am a fish with a long tail and small fins.

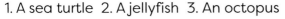
1. A sea turtle 2. A jellyfish 3. An octopus
4. A crab 5. An eel